The Sacrament of Reconciliation for Children

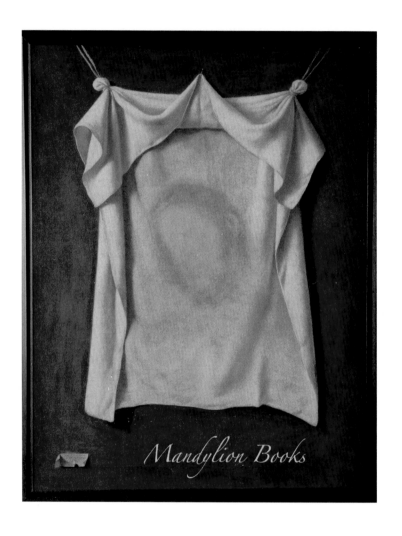

Mandylion Books

NIHIL OBSTAT, May 1, 2015
Reverend James M. Dunfee, STL
Censor
Diocese of Steubenville, Ohio

The author wishes to express deepest gratitude to Sofia Cavalletti, Gianna Gobbi, Tina Lillig, Rebekah Rojcewicz, and all of her fellow catechists in The Catechesis of the Good Shepherd for this beautiful work, which inspired every word in this book.

All of the artwork reprinted in this book is in the public domain and is used under a creative commons license. Notes on the artwork and attributions can be found in the back of the book.

All Scripture passages are taken from the New Revised Standard Version (NRSV) of the Bible.

CONTENTS

A NOTE FOR PARENTS AND CATECHISTS

Though the temptation to hurry is very great, when you are working on this book with a child or a group of children, please proceed as slowly as you possibly can. You may want to read the book one page (or even one paragraph) at a time, savoring the words from Scripture or from the rite, wondering about them together with the children. The Scripture texts and the prayers from the rites are very rich and contain much mystery. Allow for long periods of silence. If you are able, you may want to light a candle before you read the words of Jesus. When you touch the lit match to the candlewick, you might remind the children of Jesus' words: "I am the light of the world."

And though it's a very difficult thing to do, please try not to correct the children if they seem to have made a mistake. Instead, lead them back to the sources and allow them to grow into these mysteries at their own pace. You could address errors with these words, "Or maybe Jesus meant something else? Let's read it again and see what we think." If you feel as if the children are overlooking something important, try not to tell them about it. Very gently lead them back to Christ's own words. Allow Christ to teach. And most important, listen very carefully to the children, try to savor their words, and keep them in your heart to ponder later. Even when a child says something that seems completely unrelated to the discussion at hand, sometimes when we take more time to consider his or her words, we suddenly see amazing connections. These eye-opening moments are so precious! Through the children's insights our own faith can take amazing leaps. And there is a strong Scriptural basis for the practice of listening very closely to the children; Jesus told his disciples, "Truly, I say to you, unless you change and become like children, you will never enter the kingdom of heaven" (Matthew 18:3).

1. WHO ARE YOU, LORD?

The people who walked in darkness have seen a great Light
(Isaiah 9:2)

Who is Jesus?

A little over two thousand years ago, God did something completely new and marvelous. He sent his Son, Jesus, to walk the earth as a human being.

God chose Israel as the birthplace for his Son. For centuries, God had been preparing the people of Israel to receive the greatest gift ever given to humankind. He had promised to send a savior, a great king, a wonderful counselor, the Prince of Peace. The people of Israel had prayed and waited in great hope. Like all peoples, they had experienced moments of great darkness and moments of light.

When Jesus spoke and taught, ate and prayed, overcame storms and demons and all kinds of human diseases, the people who witnessed these things were amazed. Even though they had been waiting for so long for God to deliver them from pain and darkness, when Jesus stood before them, many did not understand who he was. Even those who were very close to him, who loved him, who were so hungry to hear his words that they left everything to be with him all the time, who knew for certain that he was the one God had promised, even these close friends of Jesus did not understand many of the things Jesus said and did.

They asked him a very strange question:

"Who are you, Lord?"

The Light of the World, the Good Shepherd

The answers that Jesus gave to his friends sometimes left them more confused! He once said, "I am the Light of the world." How could a person be the Light? What kind of light could Jesus mean? His friends wondered and wondered over these questions. They discussed these words of Jesus with each other and prayed to God for understanding.

At another time, Jesus said, "I am the good shepherd." There had been so many shepherds in the land of Israel. Some of those shepherds were very holy people. Abraham, Moses, and King David all tended flocks of sheep. But Jesus didn't own any animals. What did he mean when he called himself a shepherd? Where were his sheep?

Perhaps we can listen to his words to find the answer:

"The good shepherd calls his own sheep by name and leads them out. When he has brought out all his own, he goes ahead of them, and the sheep follow him because they know his voice. They will not follow a stranger, but they will run from him because they do not know the voice of strangers... I came that they may have life, and have it abundantly.

"I am the good shepherd. The good shepherd lays down his life for the sheep. I know my own and my own know me, just as the Father knows me and I know the Father. And I lay down my life for the sheep. I have other sheep that do not belong to this fold. I must bring them also, and they will listen to my voice. So there will be one flock, one shepherd" (John 10:3-5, 10b-11, 14-16).

Who are these sheep, whose names are always on the lips of the good shepherd and whom Jesus loves so much? How do they recognize his voice? Is there anything Jesus would not do for his sheep? He cares for them, he feeds them, he shelters them and keeps them safe from harm. He even lays down his life for them. He gives his whole self for these sheep. Who are these beloved sheep?

The True Vine

Another time, Jesus told his closest friends:

"I am the true vine, and my Father is the vine grower. Abide in me as I abide in you. Just as the branch cannot bear fruit by itself unless it abides in the vine, neither can you unless you abide in me. I am the vine, you are the branches. Those who abide in me and I in them will bear much fruit, because apart from me you can do nothing" (John 15:1, 4–5).

With these words, Jesus tells us who he is and who we are. But what can it mean to "abide" or *live in* in Jesus? How do we "bear fruit" and what sort of fruit is it? We know it is a fruit that can only grow when we are connected to Jesus in the same way a branch forms part of a vine. When a branch remains on a living vine, it shares a vital substance with the whole plant. What is inside a vine that brings life to all the branches? What must the branch receive from the roots and the work of the leaves in order to bear fruit? What will happen to the vine when one branch is damaged or torn off?

A little later Jesus gives us a clue about how to remain in him: "As the Father has loved me, so I have loved you. Abide in my love" (John 15:9). Love binds us to Jesus and to one another. Love is as important to our lives as the blood that flows inside our bodies.

Jesus makes this clear when he says, "If you keep my commandments, you will abide in my love, just as I have kept my Father's commandments and abide in his love" (John 15: 9-10). We all remember the Great Commandment that sums up all the others:

You shall love the Lord your God with all your heart, and with all your soul, and with all your strength, and with all your mind; and your neighbor as yourself.

Who are You, Lord?

Even when the apostles had heard Jesus speak about himself, there was so much they didn't understand. On that terrible day when Jesus died on the cross, and darkness covered the sun, they thought that he had died forever. They thought that the Light would never return. When they heard that his body was no longer in the tomb, many of them thought it had been stolen. They still did not really know who Jesus is. They also did not know who they were.

It took time for the wonderful truth to dawn on them. Jesus had come back to life! And his new life was not the same as the old life he had shared with them. It was a life stronger than death. The risen life was a gift that Jesus shared with all people of all times. When he rose from death, all the branches of the true vine received his powerful, new life.

2. WHO ARE WE?

For once you were darkness, but now in the Lord you are light. Live as children of light (Ephesians 5:8).

Jesus is the Easter Light that banishes all darkness, and through his love, we too are light. We are children of light. What a marvelous reality! We are light. The words "in the Lord" also show us the reality of who we are. We can do nothing apart from God. His life within us makes us light.

The first time we received the light of the risen Jesus was on the day of our Baptism. On that day, our candle was lit from the large Easter candle and all the power and glory of Easter was ignited in our hearts. That light can never ever go out. Since that day, every time we celebrate one of the sacraments of the Church, especially when we go to Mass, we strengthen our life in Jesus. We meet the risen Jesus, our light grows stronger, and we grow in divine love.

The Parable of the Found Sheep

Now we can ask ourselves a new question. What happens when one of the beloved sheep of the Good Shepherd wanders off and is lost? How does the Shepherd feel? What does he do? Jesus told another parable to answer these questions:

"Which one of you, having a hundred sheep and losing one of them, does not leave the ninety-nine in the wilderness and go after the one that is lost until he finds it? When he has found it, he lays it on his shoulders and rejoices. And when he comes home, he calls together his friends and neighbors, saying to them, 'Rejoice with me, for I have found my sheep that was lost'" (Luke 15: 4-6).

Do you think that the Good Shepherd is angry at the sheep when he finds it? Jesus tells us how the shepherd truly feels: great joy. He sets the sheep on his shoulders to keep it safe from harm, to keep it close to his body.

God's love doesn't stop because of human weakness. How great is God's love for us! Our incapacities cannot change this fact.

What does the shepherd do after he arrives home? Does he keep his happiness to himself? No, his joy is so great that he wishes to share it with all his friends and neighbors.

But why would the sheep wander off? How would a sheep come to be lost?

The Parable of the Forgiving Father

Jesus told another parable about a father who is like the good shepherd. When his younger son asked for half of his property, the father gave it to him:

"A few days later the younger son gathered all he had and traveled to a distant country, and there he squandered his property in dissolute living. When he had spent everything... So he went and hired himself out to one of the citizens of that country, who sent him to his fields to feed the pigs. He would gladly have filled himself with the pods that the pigs were eating; and no one gave him anything. But when he came to himself he said, 'How many of my father's hired hands have bread enough and to spare, but here I am dying of hunger! I will get up and go to my father, and I will say to him, 'Father, I have sinned against heaven and before you; I am no longer worthy to be called your son; treat me like one of your hired hands.' So he set off and went to his father. But while he was still far off, his father saw him and was filled with compassion; he ran and put his arms around him and kissed him. Then the son said to him, 'Father, I have sinned against heaven and before you; I am no longer worthy to be called your son.' But the father said to his slaves, 'Quickly, bring out a robe—the best one—and put it on him; put a ring on his finger and sandals on his feet. And get the fatted calf and kill it, and let us eat and celebrate; for this son of mine was dead and is alive again; he was lost and is found!' And they began to celebrate" (Luke 15: 13–14a, 15–24).

Why would the son choose to leave his father? What made him finally "come to himself"? What does that mean, to "come to himself"? How was the father able to catch sight of his son when he was still such a long way off? Did the father punish the son for wasting all that he'd given him? Jesus tells us that the father was "filled with compassion; he ran and put his arms around him and kissed him…". How great is God's love!

Jesus tells us that the father ordered a feast to celebrate his son's return, because his son *was dead, and has come to life again.* Jesus was never lost. He never wasted any of the gifts his Father had given to him, but he was dead and he did come back to life.

Does the Father's feast to celebrate his son's return to life remind us of any celebration in the Church?

3. THE ARMOR OF LIGHT

Let us then lay aside the works of darkness and put on the armor of Light (Romans 13:12b).

The Armor of Light

What is this armor of Light? How do we put it on? We can think back to what we know about our Baptism. On that day, we were claimed for Christ by the sign of the cross. Many people traced crosses on our foreheads with their thumbs. At the very end of the Rite, the priest also made the sign of the cross over our entire bodies. That cross acts as a shield, protecting us and clothing us with light. At any moment of the day, we can make the sign of the cross, and it will give us strength and light.

We have other armor, too. We have the example of Jesus, recorded in the Bible, to teach us how to remain in his love. Jesus has also provided us with several sayings, called Maxims, that can help us to lay aside the works of darkness; they are his moral commandments:

✦ I give you a new commandment, that you love one another (John 13:34b).

✦ Love your enemies (Matthew 5:44b).

✦ Ask, and it will be given you; search, and you will find; knock, and the door will be opened for you (Matthew 7:7).

✦ Do to others as you would have them do to you (Matthew 7:12b).

✦ Be perfect, therefore, as your heavenly Father is perfect (Matthew 5:48).

✦ Enter through the narrow gate (Matthew 7:13a).

✦ You should forgive not seven times, but, I tell you, seventy-seven times (Matthew 18:22).

✦ Store up for yourselves treasures in heaven, where neither moth nor rust consumes and where thieves do not break in and steal (Matthew 6:20).

✦ Do good to those who hate you (Luke 6:27c).

✦ Whenever you give alms, do not sound a trumpet before you (Matthew 6:2b).

✦ Pray for those who persecute you (Matthew 5:44c).

✦ Why do you see the speck in your neighbor's eye, but do not notice the log in your own eye? (Matthew 7:3)

✦ Give to everyone who begs from you, and do not refuse anyone who wants to borrow from you (Matthew 5:42).

We can take any one of these Maxims and see how closely our lives reflect Jesus' precious teachings. Now we know a little better what Jesus wants us to do when he says, "If you keep my commandments, you will abide in my love, just as I have kept my Father's commandments and abide in his love" (John 15:10).

We also can recall again the Great Commandment that sums up all the others:

You shall love the Lord your God with all your heart, and with all your soul, and with all your strength, and with all your mind; and your neighbor as yourself (Luke 10:27).

We can also pray the prayer that Jesus taught us:

Our Father, who art in heaven
Hallowed be thy name. Thy kingdom come,
Thy will be done on earth as it is in heaven.
Give us this day our daily bread,
And forgive us our trespasses
As we forgive those who trespass against us.
And lead us not into temptation,

But deliver us from evil. Amen

4. THE RITE OF RECONCILIATION

The rite of Reconciliation is one of the greatest gifts that God gives to help us lay aside the works of darkness. In it we travel the same road as the younger son in Jesus' parable. Through the prayer of Absolution, we receive the strength of the Holy Spirit and the power of the cross. Jesus' victory over death destroys all our weakness and brings us to a new life, which we celebrate with great joy, at the Good Shepherd's banquet of love, the Holy Mass.

The Rite of Reconciliation Has Four Parts:

1. EXAMINATION OF CONSCIENCE

*We listen
to the Word of God*

2. CONFESSION

*We ask for God's help by
confessing our sins to a priest*

3. ABSOLUTION

*God frees us from our sins, and
gives us strength through the
gift of Absolution*

4. PENANCE

*We answer to the
Gifts of God*

In three of these moments we do something, but in one of the moments –
Absolution – God is the one who is doing something: *He is changing us.*

Let us look more closely at each of these four parts of the Sacrament
of Reconciliation:

EXAMINATION OF CONSCIENCE

We listen to the Word of God

We read the word of God: *We can choose a Maxim, or one of the parables of Jesus, and we can try to measure our lives against how Jesus teaches us to live.*

Remember that the Ten Commandments were given to the Jewish people, to try to help them stop living and behaving as slaves. When Jesus came, much later, he already expected us to live as free people and he gave us new, more challenging commandments, the Maxims, which we have already studied in this book. He also gave us a new commandment, one he repeated again and again:

Love one another as I have loved you (John 15:12b).

In our examination of conscience, we should ask ourselves how well we have loved and whether we have ever failed to love other people the way Jesus loves us. Contrition happens in our hearts when we acknowledge our failures and feel sorry for our sins.

CONFESSION

*We ask for God's help by confessing
our sins to a priest*

Act of Contrition

My God, I am sorry for my
sins with all my heart.
In choosing to do wrong
and failing to do good,
I have sinned against you,
whom I should love
above all things.
I firmly intend, with your
help, to do penance,
to sin no more, and to avoid
whatever leads me to sin.
Our Savior Jesus Christ
suffered and died for us.
In his name, My God,
have mercy. Amen.

We tell our sins to God through a priest: *The priest has been consecrated in a very special way to do the work of God. He listens with compassion to all we say.*

We say our sins out loud, to someone else, because when Jesus became flesh and walked, and talked, and listened with human ears to the troubles of the people who came to Him, He showed us that being human and being with each other matters to God; He showed us that we are all one, just as He and the Father are one. The priest offers his ears so that God can use him to be Jesus' listening heart in the world, and he will never ever tell anyone else what we say during Confession.

When we are finished confessing our sins, the priest will ask us to say an Act of Contrition, which is a prayer to God about how sorry we are for our sins and how much we want, instead, to live the way that Jesus teaches us to live.

ABSOLUTION

God frees us from our sins, and gives us strength through the gift of Absolution

God frees us from our sins and gives us strength through the *gift* of absolution: *The priest holds his hand over us, calling down the Holy Spirit to strengthen us. He makes the sign of the cross over us, to defend us from all evil.*

There is a very sacred moment in the Holy Mass when the priest lifts both hands over the bread and wine and slowly lowers them. This gesture is called the Epiclesis. The priest is praying to God with words and also with his hands. He says, "And so Father, we bring you these gifts and ask you to make them holy by the power of your Holy Spirit, that they may become the Body and Blood of your Son, Our Lord, Jesus Christ."

The priest makes a similar gesture, called the gesture of Absolution, over each person who receives the sacrament of Reconciliation. Then the priest prays the following prayer as he lowers his hand over the person who has just confessed:

God, the Father of mercies, through the death and resurrection of his Son, has reconciled the world to himself, and sent the Holy Spirit among us for the forgiveness of sins; through the ministry of the Church, may God give you pardon and peace. I absolve you from your sins in the name of the Father, and of the Son, and of the Holy Spirit. Amen.

When the priest completes this prayer, he makes the sign of the cross over the person receiving the sacrament. We are truly forgiven! What a beautiful, blessed gift. We can come often to receive this sacrament. The gift of Absolution is always available to anyone who "comes to his senses." We only need to ask for it.

PENANCE

We answer to the Gifts of God

We receive this gift with great joy and use the new strength we have received to follow the path of the Good Shepherd.

After hearing our confession and asking God to send us the gift of Absolution, the priest will ask us to do a penance, which is usually a prayer or reading from the Bible that will help us to stay on the correct path.

Prayer is our best way to respond to God's beautiful embrace of love in this sacrament. In the second picture, we see two people shaking hands. Does sin often cause a division between us and others? How can we heal that division? How can we live in peace with the other branches of the True Vine?

In the parable of the Forgiving Father, is the moment when the younger son "comes to himself" like the examination of conscience? How? Can you find other elements in the parable of the Forgiving Father that are like any of the four parts of the rite of Reconciliation?

5 GOING DEEPER

The Healing of the Paralytic Man (Luke 5:18-26)

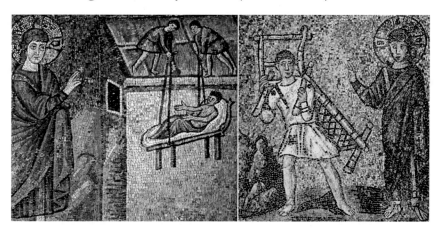

"Which is easier, to say, 'Your sins are forgiven,' or to say, 'Rise and walk'? But that you may know that the Son of Man has authority on earth to forgive sins" - he said to the one who was paralyzed - "I say to you, stand up and take your bed and go to your home." Immediately he stood up before them, took what he had been lying on, and went to his home, glorifying God (Luke 5:23-25).

In this episode from Jesus' life, we see him healing a man who is paralyzed, by telling the man, "Friend, your sins are forgiven you." There were many religious experts nearby listening, and they were shocked when Jesus said these words because they knew that only God can forgive sins. What must have gone through their minds, though, when Jesus told that man to stand up – and he was able to do it?!

From this event, we can see that being full of sin is like being paralyzed. How does sin paralyze us? How does it take away our strength to stand in the Light?

After he rose from the dead, he appeared to the apostles, who were praying in the upper room, and said, "Peace be with you." Then he breathed on them and said, "Receive the Holy Spirit! If you forgive the sins of any, they are forgiven them; if you retain the sins of any, they are retained." Jesus shares his power over sin with all priests who are consecrated to him.

31

The Parable of the Pharisee and the Tax Collector

But the tax collector, standing far off, would not even look up to heaven, but was beating his breast and saying, 'God, be merciful to me, a sinner!' I tell you, this man went down to his home justified...for all who exalt themselves will be humbled, but all who humble themselves will be exalted (Luke 18:13-14).

What attitude should we have in front of God? Why is it so important to ask for mercy? The word "justified" comes from the same word as "justice". It means to be in a right relationship with God. The Pharisee, who was an expert in religion, did many good and holy things. But did those good and holy things make him better than other people? Did he have the right to boast in front of God?

There is a moment during Mass when we are invited to beat our breasts, just as the tax collector does in this parable. This gesture is a prayer we make with our body, as we say the *Confiteor*, a prayer that puts us into the right position to be in Christ's presence:

I confess to Almighty God, and to you my
brothers and sisters, that I have greatly
sinned: in my thoughts and in my words,
in what I have done and in what I have failed to do

[we beat our breasts, three times as we say these words:]

Through my fault, through my fault, through my most grievous fault. So I ask blessed Mary, ever-virgin, and all the Angels and Saints, and you, my brothers and sisters, to pray for me to the Lord, our God.

The Healing of the Centurion's Servant

The centurion answered, "Lord, I am not worthy to have you come under my roof; but only speak the word, and my servant will be healed..." When Jesus heard him, he was amazed and said to those who followed him, "Truly I tell you, in no one in Israel have I found such faith" (Matthew 8:8 & 10).

A centurion is a Roman officer who has command of one hundred soldiers. This centurion did not follow the same religion as Jesus and his disciples, and yet he had more faith in Jesus than anyone Jesus had met.

The Church asks us to repeat the words of this Roman man during the Mass. Instead of asking for the healing of someone else, though, we ask Jesus to heal our souls. Do you remember these words? When do we say them during the Mass? How will Jesus enter under our "roofs"?

The Parable of the Rich Fool

But God said to him, 'You fool! This very night your life is being demanded of you. And the things you have prepared, whose will they be?' So it is with those who store up treasures for themselves but are not rich toward God (Luke 12:20–21)

Which of the Maxims do you think of when you read the parable of the rich fool? What does it mean to be "rich toward God"? How can we become richer in the treasures of heaven? Why, do you think, is it so wicked to store up food (more than the rich fool could ever eat)? What does the rich fool depend upon? Can any of his wealth save him from death?

Searching in the Gospels, can you find any other parables that might illustrate or help us better understand some of the Maxims of Jesus?

Icon of Christ pulling Adam and Eve from hell (copy of a fresco at Chora church), Vladimir Tamari, Acrylic on Wood, photo taken by Vladimir Tamari

Early Christian image of Christ as the Good Shepherd, 4th Century AD, Museo Epigrafico, Rome, photo taken by Kleuske

Mosaic Depicting the Punishment of Lycurgus (detail), 2nd Century AD, Musée gallo-Romain, Saint-Romain-en-Gal, France, photo taken by Carole Raddato

The Ascension (detail), 1636, Rembrandt van Rijn, Alte Pinakothek Munich, oil on canvas, photo taken by Beth Timkin

Frau mit dem Floh (detail), Georges de Latour, Musée Historique Lorrain, oil on canvas, photographer unknown

Communion of the Apostles, 1440-1441, Fra Angelico, Florence, Italy, photographer unknown

	Statue of the Good Shepherd from the Catacombs of Domitilla, 3rd Century AD, unknown sculptor, Museo Pio Cristiano, marble, photograph taken by Quodvultdeus
	The Return of the Prodigal Son (detail), Rembrandt van Rijn, Hermitage Museum, oil on canvas, photograph by Carulmare
	The Last Supper (detail), Giotto di Bondone, Scrovegni Chapel, fresco, photograph by Web Gallery of Art
	Our Lady of the Gate of Dawn, unknown artist, Gate of Dawn Chapel in Vilnius, tempura on wood, photograph by Albertus teolog
	The Good Samaritan, 1890, Vincent Van Gogh, Kröller-Müller Museum, oil on canvas, photographer unknown

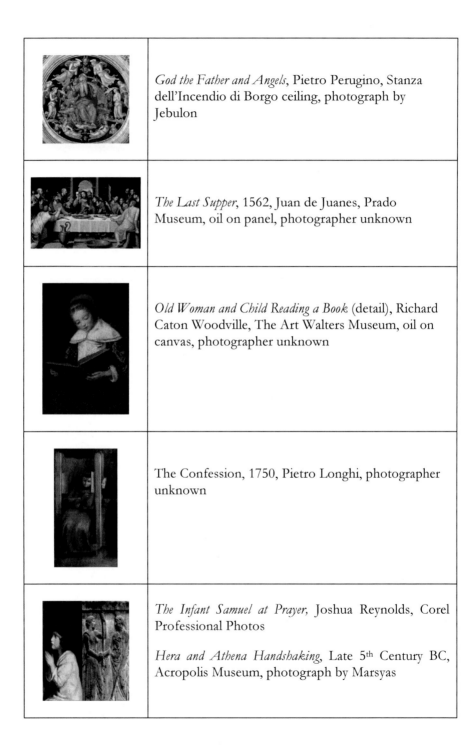

	God the Father and Angels, Pietro Perugino, Stanza dell'Incendio di Borgo ceiling, photograph by Jebulon
	The Last Supper, 1562, Juan de Juanes, Prado Museum, oil on panel, photographer unknown
	Old Woman and Child Reading a Book (detail), Richard Caton Woodville, The Art Walters Museum, oil on canvas, photographer unknown
	The Confession, 1750, Pietro Longhi, photographer unknown
	The Infant Samuel at Prayer, Joshua Reynolds, Corel Professional Photos *Hera and Athena Handshaking*, Late 5th Century BC, Acropolis Museum, photograph by Marsyas

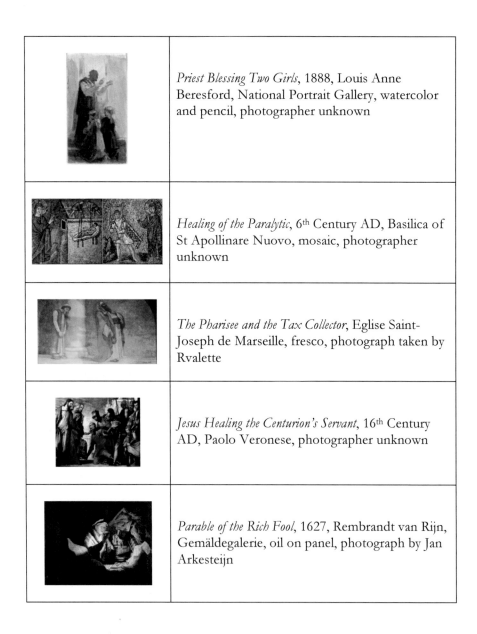

	Priest Blessing Two Girls, 1888, Louis Anne Beresford, National Portrait Gallery, watercolor and pencil, photographer unknown
	Healing of the Paralytic, 6th Century AD, Basilica of St Apollinare Nuovo, mosaic, photographer unknown
	The Pharisee and the Tax Collector, Eglise Saint-Joseph de Marseille, fresco, photograph taken by Rvalette
	Jesus Healing the Centurion's Servant, 16th Century AD, Paolo Veronese, photographer unknown
	Parable of the Rich Fool, 1627, Rembrandt van Rijn, Gemäldegalerie, oil on panel, photograph by Jan Arkesteijn

51815097R00022

Made in the USA
Columbia, SC
22 February 2019